Príncipe Vindouro

Morior Invictus

Príncipe Vindouro, a prophecy of a prince that will come to change the world.

So, you already know this will not be your usual book. Will not start by telling you my name or how do I look, neither where I come from or how my first house looked like. These kinds of details will not be important. I would rather tell you what's inside my consciousness, try to show you that we're not so different as people think they are from each other and at the same time, show you the real purpose of art.

As Tolstoy defended in 'what is art?', art should not merely be a source of entertainment or pleasure, but instead, should have a moral purpose and contribute to the development of individuals and society. So... here we go.

I'm writing because I have a secret that I found about humanity that I have been hiding for a few years and I feel that should be shared to change the way we think. I consider the secret as the answer that has long been lost from humans themselves. Many try to find it, whether in the form of theory or through the paths offered by religion, but to be honest, no one seems to be right. When they say they are, there's always something that doesn't connect and open space for people to ask some questions, that's why we call them theories or name as a religion, and even if for some that may be enough to go through life, for me, was not.

Questioning is alright… I always learn that the ones we consider the greatest minds say that we should question everything in order to learn, so I did it. Although I always felt that should be some certain that leaves no space for questions, even with philosophy and all the talk of life as no meaning, didn't make sense, they never explain nothing in concrete, questions and more questions, talking in fancy words making they're art exclusive to 'smart people'.

I should warn you first, books have never been my strength. All my life I have always loved to write but more in personal notebooks, loose sheets, supermarket receipts, whatever I found that I could put my thoughts out, always trying to find some meaning in something through a text. I remember my first text, when my father went to Africa to make some money for the family. I wrote to put some feelings out, hoping to find out the reason why I was reacting like that, so anger... Anyway, I promise that the book is not entirely about me, don't worry. I mean, obviously I want to show the paths I took to reach the secret but will not be about my boring life and my little personal problems for sure.

The story will be about my confusion in the world I was handed, perhaps the normal thing that everybody should or have been through, not understanding most of the whys and having to accept that everything must be. I didn't want 'must be', it was about my passage on the planet that I was talking about, and I would like some certainty on things, if possible.

I've always heard about intelligent people. Is everybody's dream to be a genius or at least a little bit smart, right? I was sure that I wasn't one of them, I mean… I had problems even with simple vocabulary, most of the time my mind couldn't project the idea of the word or its meaning in a clear way. Worse... never felt confident enough to state anything with certainty, thinking, certainty is something for adults, didn't know what kind of calculation they did or how they're consciousness worked to get there but at the same time I thought, 'never mind... someday I'll be an adult'.

I always loved to debate topics even though I didn't know much about things because of my age, I guess. The goal was to learn, right? I took a lot of beatings through conversations, maybe normal, I was young, so people often said I was just rebellious, indirectly mostly because they knew my father had leave the family, and maybe they were right, I kind of knew that the anger I was feeling at that time about everything was because of him, but that wasn't what led me to question the topics I'm going to address in the book though. Probably he was the fuel for, sure. You know… the need to prove something... oh well, enough about it.

The texts always included topics like science, religion, society, everything mixed in a way I couldn't explain the reason why I was talking or even writing about it. Usually, the texts arose from news I saw or books I read, the feeling that was something wrong somehow, but I had to face it, didn't have an explanation that I can give as a certain. The texts turned into confusion every time, even if I made some logical thoughts on the topics, the end of the texts was never explicit and enough for me. When I try to put them to life, through conversation, neither myself nor the person I was debating with could reach an end, prove anything, take a

conclusion and go home with a
clear brain. It was just my
viewpoint against the viewpoint of
whoever I was talking to, and
usually, only one of us was taken
as intelligent, and that was not me
because of the way I did in school.
Not that I had bad grades, just
gave up too young.

The argument that I mostly get in
this kind of conversation about
these topics was valid and logical,
although kind of silly. Was always
something like: you think
everything you read in books is
true? Well... fair enough, but at
the same time I thought, where did
you read or see that makes it true
as well? Was pointless to think
like that even though logical, but
if we humans think like that
nothing is never going to be true,

right? Think about it, we can have something to be true for three generations maximum if we think like that. Something like a war, let's imagine, a guy went and told his son about it, the son will become a dad and tell his son that grandfather went to war. Grandfather will tell stories but when he dies and the grandson tells his kids about it, and so on through generations, the kids can doubt already. I mean, they got the right to do it, using the sentence 'is everything that you read in books true?'. So, we need to kind of trust of what is written, even though, like I said before, we should question everything.

So, often, I liked to imagine how good it would be to live a life understanding every concept and every word, connecting all the dots without difficulty. I had a lot of problems in that part, simple things, for instance, when people asked me: "What do you want to do with your life?" and I answered that my dream was to do nothing, according to everyone, that couldn't be. In that case, I stopped understanding freedom, supposedly one of the most important things that exists, and no matter how much logic I applied through a text on my notebook, couldn't find a single logic to follow through my life as certain. My mind went blank most of the time, it happened with most of the concepts that we as humans consider relevant. Was making me sad... All the confusion was making my life being worst in some way, felt dumb, and hated that feeling.

Trying to learn, maybe to be smart, I wrote and wrote about everything. It still happens today, the same modus operandi, I rest my head on my left hand as if in a trance and off goes the pen, without caring about spelling errors or any rules regarding literature. It's strange… All the time making some logic's without picking a specific topic to write about it. To be honest, sometimes feels like the thoughts are coming to me in a divine way.

Well, after fifteen years of these thoughts I decided to compile most of the information I obtained and write a book that shows it all, with no fancy words or in a way that nobody can understand. I feel that humans are immensely lost in these topics that everyone claims can't be explained, so I want to show how you can do it and how simple it is, although the path can seem a little bit confusing.

If we pay attention, especially those who like to debate, most conversations develop quite a bit until both get tired and one releases a sentence like 'oh well... it's good to talk about these topics and we could stay here for hours since the debate is endless'. It always irritated me this sentence. At the time I used as well or agreed with it, often to end the conversation, I was the first usually to get tired of talking to someone who thought that something couldn't have a resolution.

An example of these conversations I'm talking about is concepts like time (later, I'll write a text taken from my personal notebooks), good and evil, etc. I gave the example of time because was one of the concepts that confused me more. I used to debate it with people, with the same ending of 'well... it's good to talk about and we could be here for hours since the debate is endless'. The debate was always about its existence, where most people could say that it didn't exist but never explain to me why in concrete. Other was good and evil, one of the most confusing as well. I used to debate the reason of why it's good or bad. Same ending. The answer as something like ''it's good because it's good'',

''because make me feel good'',
and... I notice that people couldn't
give an explanation and even say
that these are too complex things
to my mind.

 I wrote texts looking for an
explanation, in order to put an end
to these annoying conversations
when I had them. Both sides most
of the time got strong points of
view and seemed right, usually the
side against me was reality, even
if the person didn't mention I
could get the feeling, but I
thought, only one can be true, and
I wanted to know which one. Of
course, in this case, the concept of
time can be taken just as a unit of
measurement that was invented,
but there was something that I
noticed, what passes from our
birth to the day of our death.

Surely something exists. So, does time exist? Of course, it exists. Or maybe not?... Oh my… Every time was this mess with these concepts.

I wrote and rewrote, again and again, notebooks and notebooks, loose sheets and supermarket tickets. It got to the point where I would burn what I wrote every two years or so, it all sounded so confusing... I hated. The fact that I couldn't find a conclusion, no simple answer with a few words and a period at the end was making me mad. I was reading books at the same time. I thought it was likely that a brilliant mind had already discovered something, but to be honest, I didn't really know what I was looking for or how to look for. I knew there wouldn't be a book with a page that said: 'this is it'. Until one day I found the guide in a random book, during one of my visits to the library where I usually went when I had some questions to clarify or simply to entertain myself. The random book said that there were three great questions that had never been solved, and now I wanted to solve them.

Since I was a child, I was fascinated by those boards in a room filled with equations, with one person decoding everything in search of the answer to the universe. I wanted that too! but I was never good at math, so it was in these questions that I would delve and point as a starter for the journey. The questions were:

- What is the purpose of life?

- What is the nature of consciousness?
- What is the origin of the universe and what is our place in it?

Experiences

Progress towards the secret began. I put my writing into practice in life, trying to debate everything with people (probably getting too annoying). The one text that I most defended was one of the notebooks that I wrote before, when I was just writing for being mad, called: 'social credibility'. I approached the topic from a perspective where each human had their credibility in society based on a belief. I mixed with some things I was feeling in my life, and to give some context, on how that notebook started, I was expelled from a school for no apparent reason. The teacher just didn't like me and... that was it. It was unbelievable… I was mad at the time, trying to talk with the director of the school and a social worker but nothing happened… The solution they gave me was continue the course (where, if the teacher in question fails me, I fail the whole course), leave or change curse and start everything again. I couldn't believe it…

I focused on my notebooks of course, I wanted to believe that everything happens for a reason like people usually say. Couldn't explain it very well, I had a good feeling about this notebook to start the journey to find the answer. The path needs to start from somewhere and normally, my way of doing it was choosing something as the answer. The answer that I chose was:

everything is a belief. After the choice, my trick was writing about it and trying to break the reasoning that I made until there. Most of the answers that I chose didn't last much... Usually, after a few days, I could see I was wrong. In this case, couldn't call everything a belief I thought... Beliefs are not taken as something real, and reality was always the one ruining all my answers. In this answer, of everything being a belief, it was the only thought that made me wrong though, even if the most complicated and silly to be questioned. So, even if it doesn't point out for a good start, obviously, I still decided to try this one as an answer.

I was confident... I kind of knew that all conversations were likely to end with that sentence 'oh well… was good but… no end and we could go for hours…' so, I used that in my advantage, to hide the fact that I didn't have a full explanation. Hopefully, with these conversations, some logic will show up to break the reasoning, although it was strange because I didn't know if I want it to or not. I mean… who wants something that can ruin the plan?

I'm going to show a few examples of these conversations, with no timeline (since I'm awful with that) that occur in my life making me go deeper into this research, since, as you are going to see, it fuels the idea of everything being a belief, or at least, show's that could be the right path to obtain the answer and something worth to be question.

I'll start with this one:

I was in a coffee, having a conversation with a friend of my mother, we were discussed the topic of psychology because there were two people in the area where we live that people consider as 'crazy'. She is or was (not sure if retired) a psychologist. She defended her profession, of course, claiming that they were like that because they had a brain disease, one day, according to her, their brain simply gets damaged.

I argued that it was nothing more than a belief they had gained with time because everyone had it in the first place (I claimed that because I knew how their family treat them and how everybody in the city did the same treatment), but she claimed that it wasn't true, it was because of 'this and that'. I argued back, it was true! because of 'this and that'. The conversation developed, a few hours passed, and a story that she told in the middle of an argument, trying to prove her point, caught my attention.

It was about a patient who went to the psychiatric clinic where she worked, the problem was that he believed he was possessed by Christ. Proceeding, she told me about the treatment they gave him there, the trick was that they had a shock therapy session and filmed it. After, they called the patient to another room and showed him what they had recorded, convincing him that in the moment of one of the shocks

Christ left. To everyone's surprise... the patient was cured. Well, she didn't prove her point. Actually, she was making me right, but I didn't bother to continue the conversation. She continued, but my mind turned off when I heard that story. Usually happens a few times, my mind turning off from the real world, my girlfriend tells me I'm going away. Anyway... I felt in that conversation that the text of social credibility was coming to life, I didn't like it, in fact I hated it when someone felt superior, especially because of that text that I was seeing as 'the truest' to be followed. I had what I wanted from this conversation, however, I was still struggling to explain myself. I had to believe, in this case, that there were real diseases, so it couldn't be everything just a belief, and again, here it was reality to ruin my plans.

Well, I'll proceed with another conversation that gave me strength to keep going. It was something like this:

I was in a classroom, having a conversation with a teacher, we were discussing a project that we were doing where we had to describe an image. By turns we had to say what we see without what we think it is, then, say what we think it is.

My image was of a person lying on a bed with two others sitting next to him. The person lying down had tubes connected to his body that were connected to a screen, and the two people sitting had controllers in their hands. When it was my turn to say what I thought it was I said I thought it was a patient in a hospital bed, connected to a heart monitor, and the two people sitting were an angel and death with the controllers connect to the screen so it's as if they're playing for the patient's life.

The presentation of the projects continued until it was time to receive our evaluations. I received a very low grade and everyone else received a maximum grade (since it was an easy project). I asked why, of course. The response I received from the teacher was that the image did not feature an angel but rather God. Apparently, you could tell from God's white beard and typical hairstyle she said.

Hm… I thought to myself… what could I say without being asked to leave?...

I simply protested by saying it wasn't fair, it was supposed to be about what I think it is and not what she thinks it is. As expected, this sparked a heated debate. She took her side, I took mine, once again my writing came to life, I started talking while trying to show my idea about everything being a belief. I tried to show her without offending any religious beliefs, was never my goal to feel superior, just wanted to show my point of view. I asked if it wouldn't be more logical to have the devil on the other side since God was on one of the sides (was almost impossible by the draw to

say it wasn't death, you know…
black dress and a scythe). I
proceeded asking as well if it was
against the rules for an angel to
have a beard, I wasn't familiar
with their regulations so, shouldn't
hurt to ask. I said that, for me,
God wasn't even white. I tried
everything to show my point even
using one of her favorite writers,
Camões, and I pointed out that the
image we got from him is all
speculation. But nothing... I was
asked to leave. She also wrote a
note in the teacher's notebook that
I couldn't accept my evaluation. It
was frustrating...

Possible fair. I was talking about
my beliefs without being able to
explain them clearly, and that
made the person in the debate mad
about it. Belief seems to be not

enough, but to that day, no one had put forward a convincing argument that breaks the reasoning, so belief still was the closest thing I had to an answer.

So, down to the last conversation. To be honest I would like to share more, was unbelievable how many I had like this, but I didn't have the space to fill my memory with all of them since were too many. I was always busy writing them, that's true, but like I said before, everything turns into ashes so, not much to do now. The last one I'm going to share it happened like this:

I was in a bar, having a conversation with a guy, we were discussing all kinds of topics, just seeing time past. He knew I enjoyed a good conversation so

often came to me to talk about
something, always with a curiosity
tone mixed with some teasing.
 At that time, I had just finished
reading Plato's book, Theaetetus.
My brain was filled with ideas
because of it, a little bit confusing
to explain but somehow, I could
connect the book with the writing
I was doing before even reading it
and that made me felt that I was
on a good path, but the book
didn't have a conclusion that I
could give as a certain because,
you know, philosophers...
 I kept talking and talking, trying
to show the idea of everything
being a belief that I had, but the
response I received was "oh... you
come to me to talk about
knowledge? I'm a civil engineer".
It was as if he was saying 'I have

nothing to learn from you', or like I didn't even have the right to talk about these things, and…
shouldn't, but sometimes made feel a little sad, dumb.

He knew I had only completed the seventh grade, so did I, maybe that's why the dumb part, and this was just one of many attacks I received due to that. Maybe it is fair all these arguments that I get... just had a feeling about everything, not an explanation. I swear I really wanted to be able to explain it, but whenever I tried to put forward an idea, it only led to more confusion because reality, again, couldn't be just a belief and there were things like good and evil as well that… never mind.

I tried... I wrote a thousand arguments, there were examples like the true time, like I mentioned before, you know… what it passes between birth and death, and I couldn't just put as a belief. I was sure that I born, I was sure that I'm going to die. It is the truth, reality.

Therefore, conversations as you can see didn't go well for me most of the time but I had as well a few collections of articles or movies that boosted the research. I promise not to be annoying with things that fuel the research. After this chapter I will jump to what matters, but I feel these conversations or collections are important, or at least, interesting.

I'll start with that one time that I read an article about a girl. It was written that every day she felt exhausted despite doing nothing, so on a visit to the doctor, to see what was going on, was diagnosed with autism. The reason she felt exhausted every day was that she used her energy to pretend to be a normal person. I found it strange, for some reason, although I am not an expert on the subject to go into it. I was concentrating on the term 'normal person' though. Although I understand the term, and can remove the prejudice from it, the story itself shows that there are certain rules we need to obey to be considered a 'normal person', like it was not natural, and somehow, I was connecting this article with the conversation that I had with the psychologist, in the beginning of it, when we discuss about the 'crazy' people. I was connecting this as well with stories that I read about kids that grow up in the jungle, we got a few, these kids learn to be the animal they close to when they grow. We got stories of a few that grow up with monkeys, wolves, between dogs, and it pointed out to be just a belief this thing of being human. Don't get me wrong, I'm not disrespectful enough to say that the disease in this case (autism) it's just a belief, of course there was still reality but… oh well… just thoughts…

I felt the same (a connection between) while watching movies like 'Split' or 'Life is Beautiful'.

'Split' is a movie that portrays a character with an extreme form of dissociative identity disorder (DID). However, the portrayal of DID in the movie is not an accurate depiction of the disorder, but in a way, I always felt that connects with the answer that I chose: everything is a belief. I mean… the real condition shows how one person can have two or more distinct personalities and these different identities may have distinct ways of speaking, and unique names, ages and genders. Again, I'm not disrespectful to say that the disease doesn't exist, just saying that this fuels the research.

'Life is beautiful', it portrays a father in the times of war, it was sent to a concentration camp, and in there, he uses his humor and imagination to shield his son from the horrors of it, convincing his son that it's all just a fun game.

These movies left me thinking for a few days. Not because it's hard to process, I was just thinking of how fascinating it is that a belief completely changes the person's mind. In 'life is beautiful' gets to the point of what for a few was being a horror, for that kid, was fun, and I know… we could think about that was possible because is just a child and children are more vulnerable in this kind of things, but… My mind started to go away… Through different eras… thinking about, for instance, weren't the ones who passed through this planet until now also deceived? As if humanity was the father in the movie and people the son. I was thinking... we come to the planet, someone tells us what is wrong or right, what is what, etc. Some see it as a fun game, others, horror, and again, it gives me the feeling of everything being a belief.

I was feeling lost… I'm going to repeat myself but, reality… what a nightmare…

I was focused on trying to clarify the sentiment. So, I get a clear notebook in my desk, some loose sheets of paper, a dictionary and a collection of encyclopedias from my grandfather and start to point out things and their meanings while at the same time writing a few more texts.

I went to the dictionary as a starter to see what humans understand by the term belief, and belief is:

- an attitude of mind in which someone (with varying degrees of certainty) admits something as true.
- a deep conviction (in

something) that does not
derive from rational analysis.
The first definition aligned with
what I had been thinking. An
attitude of mind in which someone
admits something as true, where
the degree of certainty, obviously,
is going to vary on the individual.
But let's face it, the freedom as an
individual we always give as
unlimited, however, in this
society, we got things that are
allowed to give as a belief and
others that don't, because of
reality I guess, and that's why we
call it belief...
The second definition states that it
does not derive from rational
analysis. Not going to lie, made
me a little sad this meaning. It
meant that belief might not be the
answer I was looking for, maybe it

wasn't up to me to explain or even understand because it didn't derive from rational analysis. I was willing to try though. I had nothing to lose, what's the worst thing that could happen? Worst case scenario I learn something, right? time needed to pass anyway.

I started thinking again about how humans (especially grownups) could be so sure about something. I knew, or I thought I knew, the term equality, so my frustration was: what makes someone so sure that they can assert something without fear or confusion? I thought about intelligent people again. Perhaps there is a moment when they know something to the point where they can assert it confidently and that kept me

searching for my certain as well.
 There was a question that constantly lingered in my mind from the book that I couldn't stop thinking about it, Theaetetus. Socrates asked Theaetetus if he could explain what SO (the first two letters of his name) meant. The answer was that is an S and an O. Continued, Socrates asks if that was the explanation he gave for the syllable and soon as Theaetetus said yes, Socrates asked for the explanation of the letter S.
 It fascinated me...
 The thought showed how we could have full knowledge of a whole (word) but not full knowledge of an element (letter). Using other words, Socrates gave the example of a car, it would be

like having full knowledge of the whole (car) but not full knowledge of an element (piece), and it might be acceptable for an average person, but someone had to have full knowledge to invent the first car, right? The idea was confusing when it was about language. I knew when it comes to theory it's the same, something we did through generations, but the point of this example I think it was to show that is an invention.

I spend a few days thinking… I had to find something more to clarify these thoughts, maybe search for a book that shows how language was created. So, I went to the library like usual. Nothing was certain, everything I found was theories. It wasn't enough for me. The worst is that I had in my mind the thought of, how can I even think about all these things if I can't even explain what I use to do it? The subject of language was making me lose my sleep, making logical deductions all the time, feeling like nothing is ever going to be resolved. Until I come to one that I thought it has is logic and could help.

Going to seem evil but, hypothetically speaking, if a baby were locked in a room where they didn't hear any language, he wouldn't learn to speak, right? Not even with two or three babies, if neither of them knows, is impossible to develop the language as we know it, would take generations and generations, and I know… that's how supposedly happen, this is just to prove the point, again, that it was an invention.

Ironically, later, I found a story in a theory of language book that talks about a prince who conducted the experiment that I put as hypothetical. His goal was to find the true language of humans so he could be devoted to it since was supposed to be the true one. The children never spoke. Was written that they make sheep sounds since the place was close to a farm with a few sheep. It was not a surprise, at least for me.

I delved deeper into this matter. I was thinking, my thoughts are organized and got into sense by an inner voice (as I'm showing with this sentence or with the thinking in the whole book), so it made me wonder, does that inner voice come with humans? I was certain that not. In order to have a notion how it sounds is necessary to hear language first. I'll give an example: I noticed that deaf people are accompanied by speechlessness or when they speak, I could immediately tell that they are not knowledgeable of how it sounds. Then I found out, not even in dreams, I read an article where the person, a deaf mute, explained his communication when he dreamt. I found the answer amusing, everyone used sign language. That means that they don't have an inner voice as someone 'normal' and their thinking (as we know it, inner voice) occurs in a different way, they can make associations, but they use the same understanding that just becomes possible after the creation of language.

I know that thinking is not just about the inner voice, includes more things, and that's where my curiosity kicks in, so I start to wonder, is it possible that we create thinking?

Reasoning ≠ Thinking

Science asserts that humans are the only rational animals and now, with all these thoughts, it was something I was prepared to question. I always thought it unfair that we humans consider other animals as irrational, making us look like a superior species. I don't know… there's a few things that they do that I always feel is kind of wrong to classify as mere instincts.

I consulted the dictionary on reasoning and thinking before delving too deep into these thoughts.

On reasoning, it said:

- to use reason to deduce, judge, or understand; to link

ideas logically; think.
Thinking, it said:
- to use reason to deduce,
  judge, or understand; to link
  ideas logically; reasoning.
After seeing it, I deduced that
humans would benefit more if the
words were not included within
each other, and thinking could
have the same meanings, besides
reasoning, but at the same time I
felt that thinking was something
else.
I thought it would be better to
state that every animal can reason
whereas think is exclusive to
humans. I'll make an example to
clarify the reason I thought of that.
Zebras, when being hunted,
sacrifice the little ones so the
grownups can run. I was assuming
that they were not thinking and

just reasoning the moment. I mean… can't call it an instinct the fact they are choosing the one who goes easily without a fight, or the fact they know if one goes the others can get out of there. We can say that running from danger is an instinct, but not the choices they made.

In other hand, thinking the moment will be when we use our inner voice. Taking the case of the zebras again, if it was humans, would think that is a sacrifice and that is bad, etc.

I don't know if it helped. Either way I was assuming that since it was logical. I decided to go back to the meanings, run a few more logical deductions through my mind. I start to wonder if animals also used reason to deduce, judge or understand. I mean, it was fair to agree that they did not do the part of linking thoughts logically and thinking since for that they already need notions like time, good and evil, … (like I write in the example of zebras).

So, I imagined a hunt. Evaluating the right moment to act is a judgment, right? Now forgetting the hunt, if there is a judgment of things there is comprehension, and that will lead to the use of reason to deduce, right? It seemed correct, although at the time I thought it wasn't worth going against science, I would be entering into facts and as it's said in Portugal "there are no arguments against facts". I had arguments... I could explain them, my problem was, developing too deep always lead me to the point of reality, and I couldn't break it down. Didn't want my discoveries to be a theory, it would just be another one, I wanted something more conclusive, something that couldn't be denied by logic, the truth, I guess.

The days were passing, I had in mind the division between reasoning and thinking, mixed with the thoughts about language, and not forgetting, the idea that everything is a belief as well.

I start to imagine things, through some logic and visions, and I get to one to initiate the next step. I was imagining humans in their primitive side, was right to say that they were once only rational animals (in order of the division that I wrote above), learning from others and guided by instincts and memories to solve problems (as we designate irrational animals today). I thought… it was like this until the invention of some advanced communication for sure, and I was calling advanced and not just communication because communication can be found in other animals as well, what made unfair to treat just as communication and felts right to say advanced.

Now, by advanced I mean mostly speech and writing. I started these thoughts after I consulted the dictionary on reasoning and thinking, and the word that made me wonder was: understanding.

My train of thought was: to understand something you need to have something to understand, right? When we come to the world, especially these days, there's already something to understand, a way of being, but this something somehow must be created, right? When I say this, I'm not saying that we need to create things that exist by themselves. I'm saying that we create the words and meanings that can shape our understanding. For instance, as we designated, irrational animal, they can look to a river and… nothing. We humans look, know that is a river, know that it flows toward the ocean, etc. Felt strange soon as I noticed that. That's what we humans call knowledge, or at least the logic point towards, and it became worse when I was starting to wonder a lot about it. I know that can look like overthinking, to be honest kind of was, but I felt that was something strange about it. By my logic was fair to assume that most of the knowledge is passed by communication (like I point it out that when we come to the world there's already things to understand) so I searched about communication in general.

• Communications

Science defends that communication most likely began with early human beings through vocalization and gesturing, evolving naturally, until we develop speech, that obviously will evolve naturally as well. In my mind didn't make sense... using gestures or small sounds sounded wrong. For me, logical, even a primitive gesture requires an interpreter (that needs to have knowledge how to interpret the moment) and someone to interpret (that need to have knowledge of that interpreting mode). It was almost impossible to create a logic that explains the beginning of that advanced communication, but everything points out to be an invention.

I thought that it made sense to think that it needed to be trustful and peaceful in the beginning because if it wasn't, nothing would have started (although I notice that later can be taught in a peaceful way as well, but not necessarily).

I was a little bit confused to be honest, was messy to think how they created advanced communication without a tool like speech or writing. For example, simply naming the sun, if one made a gesture or simple sound, the other one wouldn't understand anything since they didn't have the act of naming yet, right? Even if they point to it, and make the gesture or the sound at the same time, how someone can connect to being the name? It's confusing I know...

That led me to look up communication in the dictionary, as I thought it was more likely that there would be misunderstandings as there were (at least for me) with reasoning and thinking.

Communication is defined as:
- the exchange of information between individuals through

speech, writing, a common
code or behavior.

I analyzed each of the meanings.
Through the speech I had already
seen that it couldn't have been at
the beginning and writing even
less so. A common code or
behavior, however, piqued my
curiosity.

Getting back just a little bit, to
when I wrote that humans once
were merely rational creatures
(without an inner voice and acting
by instincts) and when I wrote as
well that knowledge was passed
most by communication. Now, as
I divide reasoning from thinking
(with the example of zebras), I
also divide communication into
two types:

- The natural one:
  - Emerges with any animal.

- The advanced one:
- Don't emerge with any animal. Created by humans.

I made some assumptions about natural communication, perhaps would help I thought. I started to see if I could identify what differentiated it from the advanced one. Using fire as an example, imagine the two beings that are at least necessary to create it. Suppose that one of them burns themselves gaining the knowledge that fire burns. Now, how can they transmit this knowledge without the advanced one? They can't.

This meant, by logic, that natural communication is kind of useless because you cannot pass your experience. In the example of fire, a lioness mother, if she got burned and now has the knowledge that fire burns, cannot convey this notion to her offspring, the offspring needs its own experience in order to gain the knowledge that fire burns. The best that the mother can do is use natural communication to prevent the offspring from burning itself, like grabbing and moving away or rowing as a universal sound. Don't seem enough though, the mother can never explain the reason or a notion like burn even if already burn herself.

In other hand the advanced communication seems more useful since you can share experience. In the example of fire again, if a human mother got burned and has the knowledge that fire burns, can convey to her offspring that fire burns, explaining even the

consequences. The offspring no longer needs experience because can imagine and even teach the next generation, through advanced communication, that fire burns and the meaning of burn, etc.
 Seem right…
 Trying to conclude these thoughts and make the divisions official I checked one last time the meanings of reasoning and thinking in the dictionary, I assumed that on reasoning, only think was out of place. My logic was, other animals can also link ideas logically since, as I saw on the example, a mother can take the offspring away from the fire. Meaning that she can connect fire and burn. Another example, the warthog, as I saw one time in a documentary, the mother makes a

lot of holes in the ground and makes the little ones go in every single one in order to get the smell. After, they are going to live normally until the moment that the lion decides to hunt. When that happens, the little ones hide in random holes, being up to the lion to find out in which one they hide. I mean… that seems like link ideas logically.

The reason that I make the division is, seem more logical, sounds fairer and less egocentric, and opens space to explain and give as a certain that think is an invention and not really what we think it is.

In that time felt that my research was going great.

I don't know... felt like I was on the right track regardless of whatever the destination of the path was. Not sure that was leading to the answer, but it was logical, and was like a lullaby to my mind. Confused, sure... Sometimes I was having second thoughts. From the beginning there was that clash with reality so what was I expecting? The deeper I delved into the research the more the clash occurred on my subconscious. Was stuck in there the fact that reality is what it is, so what was the point? There was no point in searching for anything. Even if reality doesn't explain itself a few times, it presents itself, and that was enough, I guess...

I began to consider giving up...

However, I proceeded...

Perhaps because the feeling was strong or maybe... just bored...

Concepts

After what I had exposed, I still wanted to affirm that everything was just a belief, but to be a scientific thing, without reality included, couldn't be everything so, couldn't be.

Often, I admitted to myself to see if I could get somewhere, okay… things are real, but the question pops up in my mind: how could we reach this understanding?

I wrote a lot about some concepts through the path, to see if I could find some way to break through and make everything logical. Some concepts such as infinity, nothingness, time or space, etc. When I wrote about it, logic did not match up with each other's, and for me, illogicality was the worst on my writing.

I had questions like, how did we reach the understanding of something like nothingness if it doesn't exist? It seemed that in order of the simply opposite (since we have what exists) but at the same time I felt it could only be a belief that we create with language, with the thinking that I had already assumed we created as well. I mean, things like infinity or time, for instance, were easier to imagine how we reach the understanding, since it's hard to assume as something that is not real. But nothingness… the point of it is that is not real since doesn't exist, right?...

Time was passing… I was entertaining myself writing about

these concepts. Confused, I decided to go back to the dictionary to see if I could clarify my mind and find a few meanings interesting enough for me to be curious about.

I searched for infinity, that is:
- that which has no limits
- time and space taken as absolute
- (figuratively) - God, the absolute, the eternal

In here I notice the same simple opposite. That which has no limits meaning that we first create the limits and then we could take them away and obtain infinity. Then, I noticed the term "absolute", means that which exists independently of any conditions. That was fair... I could understand the sense of it even if it goes away from my answer, so, again, I start to struggle.

The question remains: how did we reach understanding to the point of being knowledge and give the same knowledge as a certain? Perhaps something about knowledge that I miss. As humans we learn we are smart, that knowledge is certain, is real. So, I went back to the dictionary to check knowledge, I wanted to see if I could find some way to break through, so I leave a little bit the meaning of concepts aside, and found out that knowledge is:

- a direct relationship that one has with something
- a notion, information, or experience.

Was good I thought. It correlated with the example of fire that I wrote down and showed in the previous chapter. Although I disagreed with the dictionary on knowledge on a few things. First it states, a direct relationship that one has with something, makes sense as it points as an experience per say (like the example of fire, the mother lioness). The word information was good as well. That leaves notion in the case, and here is where I most disagree. Notion could not be considered as knowledge, and in order to not be wrong I went in the dictionary, and notion is:

- Simplistic knowledge or shallow understanding of something
- Knowledge of something through intuition; idea

This makes the point stronger. I

made some logic like: when a lioness shows the offspring how to hunt, the offspring get a notion but not real knowledge, what we call as well as learning the theory. But I wonder, if a human mother teaches the kid about something that doesn't exist, like nothingness for instance, is considered as knowledge when he knows what nothingness is, right? I wonder because some concepts that I learn, or we humans learn, don't exist and we still take them as real knowledge even though everything points towards to be all just imagination, belief.

I wrote down a note to myself. It states that, through experiences we can get real knowledge, occur from a clash with reality, like fire burns. Through notion the dictionary says we can get a simplistic knowledge but should be even considered having the word knowledge in it? we got no experience... In the same note I wrote an example as well to explain better and it states: death, we say that we have the knowledge of what it is, even got a name for it, but we (humans) never had the experience, at least the ones alive, and the dead ones… can't transmit the information through communication, right? So, to be honest, we don't know anything about it.

It was getting difficult even if all my logic seemed right. I started to think about what I had until now. I felt close to an answer because even if it looks messy in here, in my head, was starting to be clear. I was now focused on clarifying concepts like good and evil. I mean, that influenced all my life, and for certain, society since they're the basis of everything we do, we do it in order of 'because it's good' we don't do it or avoid doing 'because it's evil'. I believed I knew what these concepts were, but I continued with the research knowing that what I knew for sure always turned out to be wrong, or at least a misunderstanding, since the dictionary goes most of the time against logic itself.

Absolute

I thought I was getting the right idea out of all this, and with a little bit of patience, things were going to connect. So, I proceeded as promised the investigating about good and evil.

Before going to the dictionary, as I always did, I made I question to myself. Could science explain good and evil? I knew that it could provide variants of explanations, but the concept itself seemed to be impossible to explain, that's why philosophers love it.

I came up with some logic. For instance, I've always been in favor of not littering, sometimes if I saw someone doing it or if there was excessive garbage lying around, I

would pick it up and dispose of it properly. I called that 'doing the good thing', the 'correct thing to do'. A thought also came to me, and it was an impertinent question: according to whom?
 It wasn't a matter of applause. Answering that 'made me feel good' will lead me to myself, and there was a reason why I was investigating this. Then I asked some people, atheists, and the answer I got was "according to my conscience", that will lead to the same answer of that made me feel good. Was not enough. It sounded wrong, I couldn't understand why they spoke about their conscience in the third person. It will be like punching someone and saying, "it wasn't me, it was my hand". Didn't make sense, but let's

assume, okay, it is according to their conscience. So, I proceed imagining, a confrontation between me who picks up litter from the ground, and the person who litter in the first place. In a one-on-one situation, it is fair to say that neither of our views are valid, both individuals should have the space to be free, their own vision. However, when we put our (let's call it) global consciousness to work, the definitions are already here when we born, so it is more likely that I would emerge victorious for doing the right thing. So, I can conclude that could be about me (conscience), but it is like a program where we act, without questioning, on the pre-existing definition of good and evil that we already have. I mean, I know, like I said, that philosophers love it, however, they never can conclude anything because each mind has its own freedom to think and like I say in the beginning, leaves space for questions.

To stay logical in this topic, I thought about the same question posed to a religious person. According to whom? the answer I would get is, according to God. Makes more sense, not going to lie, in religion (as far as I understand it), God sets the rules and doing good is linked to things like entering heaven due to the judgment that God will make. Made more sense even if the fact of not questioning. I mean, it's God we are talking about.

So, the question remains. Outside

of religion, according to whom? Who is judging? Even using the most drastic example, killing someone, that has a consequence of going to prison as it is considered evil, incorrect. But... who considers it so without God? I know that is a rule but the ones who did it were according to what? What if they were atheists? They couldn't explain the question according to whom, so most probably the rule wouldn't even be born. The judgment would arise from human beings and philosophically, everyone has the right to his own thoughts, and we are too many to make a statistic each generation to decide. I could think about common sense as well, but common sense is the opinion of a whole and the same question will appear since by logic it is the same: what is that whole based on?

Everything seemed to lead to good and evil being religious concepts, but at the same time, I thought, shouldn't be (and it's not in these days) necessary to believe in God to know that killing is wrong, although looks like. The reason I say this is that outside of religion, no higher power is judging, and to be honest, things seem to get a little bit out of sense. (I want to clarify that I used the example of killing because is the peak of evil).

Now, my next step was dividing society into two:

- religious people:
- who believe in God and good and evil will be according to

him.

- atheists:
- who believe in infinity and good and evil will be according to it.

I'll put infinity on atheists' side just because in the dictionary they put them together as well, as I saw, no specific reason, at that time I didn't assume anything as true (certain) for the atheists, but I notice they obey as well to the concept of good and evil.

To justify the division, I'll state the rule of infinity that I read, which is: "Let's think about an object of finite volume. Now, let's remove 99% of it and leave only 1%. If we repeat this process infinitely, it may approach zero but will never reach the point of being nothing.". Doing an analogy, infinity or God represents the object of finite volume that needs to be created, as 'the creation' that will make other creations possible or believable. After, we can repeat the process of creation infinitely, and at most it will approach zero but never become nothing, as I wrote that it was when we were once merely rational animals, with natural communication.

Seems right again although was hard to assume all this as the truth. I still had the idea of strange knowledge to clarify, like nothingness, as I wrote down, if a mother teaches her kid the meaning of it, we humans assume that now the kid got the knowledge, so I looked up on the dictionary, out of curiosity, and it

defined nothingness as:
- the absence, whether absolute or relative, of being or reality
- that which does not exist; nothing; zero.

I find myself disagreeing with the dictionary once again. How could it be zero? Zero already exists, like I saw on the rule of infinity that it states that may approach zero or even go through zero to minus (since its infinite) but will never reach the point of being nothing.

I began to understand...

I was up to something. This thought stayed in my head for several days, was making sense for someone to take both, infinity or God as absolute, although my inclination was more towards the infinity part because for me, infinity was not the best choice.

I proceeded, having a feeling that in the topics good and evil will find something that'll make clear. I went to the dictionary again, and in good found that is:

- (adverb) - in a pleasant, satisfactory, or convenient manner
- correctly; accurately
- favorably or fortunately
- (noun) - everything that is good, just, lawful, valuable and morally right
- virtue
- what is useful for a particular purpose; beneficial.

I noticed something constantly in my thoughts and now I found it here too: correctly. It is correct, it is incorrect, and that starts to sound strange. Again, a question that I had written down: correctly according to whom? Who judges everything that is good, just, lawful, valuable and morally right? It only made sense in religion, as I saw it before, because the answer will be according to God, but outside of religion was still out of sense.

Then I looked up evil as well. Found that it means:
- (adverb) - in a manner different from what should be; irregularly
- imperfectly
- (noun) - everything that harms, wounds, or annoys
- what is contrary to good.

Once again… couldn't stop wonder about the question: according to whom?... there's no high power for judge if you don't believe in God.

As I analyzed the meaning of both concepts, my mind went away, and out of nothing, light. I started to notice something when I thought about what I was seeing on the good side: what is useful for a particular purpose, beneficial. On the evil side: everything that harms, wounds or annoys.

Now I was mixing a thought that I had before with this one that I was having about good and evil while away, probably had it even before thinking about all this, and will be important to make this one clear. The thought is the base of most problems to be honest. Humans as a main unit. In this case, I notice that humans are the main unit on this equation, and that's why I couldn't see the answer for the question, according to whom outside of religion? First, I'll give just a little example of how humans think of themselves as the main unit in any equation. Taking as an example what we do with dogs, when we say that one human year equals seven years for a dog, making humans the main unit, and I know that can look like it makes sense because we the ones who created, but let's face it, we give it as a reality and not as a creation (maybe not specifically this one from dogs, but time for instance, for sure).

So, it was time to try to find a way to remove humans from being the main unit on the concept of good and evil, to see if I could get somewhere, and considering the question of according to whom, the answer I found possible, the 'light', was **life**.

Life is the answer not just for atheists but for religion (society as a whole).

I came up with some logic to justify the answer. Taking a rock as an example, if someone asks me if it has life, I (and everybody I guess) will say no. By logic, I have knowledge of what life is. However, if someone asks me to explain what life is, since I can identify its absence on the rock, I don't know as a certain to be honest, the best I could give is a few aspects of it. That means one thing. We don't have knowledge of what life is, the maximum we can have is a notion, and a notion as I see it through the book, shouldn't be considered as knowledge.

The notion of life came before any religion, and that's why for atheists good and evil make sense (even though people don't know how to explain).

I looked up life in the dictionary and through all the meanings I chose only two:

- the state of being alive
- the period between birth and death; existence.

I chose this two because, one the first one says, the state, and… Who states? On the second one says, the period between birth and death, existence, and the idea of the period between birth and death, the existence, was one of the major's justifications that we humans give to everything, obviously. It will be found in all concepts since they exist, so I assume that this indirectly means reality, the absolute, and once again, I faced the obstacle of reality to get to the answer by proving that everything is a belief.

I kept going... although tired of my mind being sick because I was going in circles.

It was necessary to develop a certainty without falling into theories, so I decided to move onto my biggest obstacle, reality, and as usual, I looked up reality in the dictionary trying to have a starter, and found that it means:
- the quality of what is real
- that which exists in fact
- certainty.

I thought about it for a few days to develop a logic... I was thinking about quality, in fact, certainty…

One good day, the logic I was looking for appeared. This was my last step in the research even if I didn't know it. It's a simple one but I think it reveals the answer (secret).

The logic is: imagining a classroom where a teacher points to a board with the color red on it and asks: "what is the name of this color?" If a student answers green the teacher will say that it's wrong, right? Well... in 'reality', it's not.

We humans must realize something. We call it red because we peacefully agreed and still agree to call it that, like anything else. It's not reality or a fact. It's a dream made by us, possible because of advanced communication because in silence or even with the natural one, there's no explanation, just experiences.

Nothing escapes this creation.

It may be what we call reality but that's just what we call it. It's not a law of the universe... Things can be 'real' but our understanding and the way we act in it will always be because we created a notion of life, and a notion… will always be something that we create through imagination.

And that concludes.

Everything is just a belief.

Finally

Everything became clear that night. I understood for the first time the world I was living in. Fascinated by the journey, even if complicated and confusing.

The answer was simple. I understood why I couldn't understand. I always assumed that the knowledge we share was a certain, and that blocked the possibility of understanding that it's all an invention and there's nothing to really understand, unfortunately, in what we call the universe.

That day, when everything was revealed, I shed tears of euphoria. Days passed and I couldn't sleep. It was hard to explain to the people around me, was too much to take in for someone, and honestly, to let it out. Was sad they never seemed excited as I was, always trying to find a way to 'bring me to reality', never arguing enough and doubting that it was me that found the answer that philosophers try for ages.

I still have one problem. I never know in each category should put the book in. I don't think it should be philosophy even if that is the category that most fits. I'm only justifying the world that we humans create, and I know it sounds audacious... but nothing can prove me wrong since it is only an understanding, an imagination as I saw before, and language is never going to be something I will trust from now on. Think about it… trough silence we humans can't explain nothing and as I saw before, language doesn't come with us so, I'll stick to my experiences.

 As I wrote, I'm not creating a new world or theory. I simply showed step by step how the dream of the whole works and how it was created. In the beginning, there had to be a peaceful agreement, we would not have gotten here so far in advanced communication if there was such a thing as discordance. Imagine if someone naming something, the other person just turns around, not showing interest or not being peaceful, we wouldn't even have the first meaning of something. To disagree you must first agree in a peaceful way (unconsciously) on what disagree means, after, of course, create the meaning of disagree.

Since we have a dream now, it's useful to know this information. We shouldn't fight over who is right or wrong when in the universe, nobody is.

With this book I broke reality. My goal is not to bring humanity back to nothingness but rather to show that we should not be so rigid or think that reality is an absolute truth and there's even something like an absolute truth for somebody to feel superior. Like I wrote, things can be 'real' but our understanding and the way we act in it will always be because we created a notion of life, and a notion… will always be something that we create through imagination. Every time we see, touch, hear, smell, taste, we take a meaning out of it and that meaning is imagination, just that.

Also, we should not forget that life is just a notion and is the main unit of the calculation of good and evil. Good and evil control our lives and the society we live, just need to think about… everything we do is based on if is good or bad, if it going to bring good or bad things, even the path as humanity, is for a better future.

That makes us the creators.

In modern days, we've reversed roles, we judge humans as the main unit because we forget who created advanced communication and take it as a reality. That's why, in schools, we say that (as in the example) green is wrong and do

not explain that we call red
because is just beneficial for a
connection and to make the dream
possible.

The great dream we live in arose
from that, communication, it's a
full world of words and meanings
that makes us see something that
there's not to see.

I went to the dictionary for the
last time, curious about the
meaning of imagination since we
create everything through it, and
found that it means:

- the faculty of inventing, of
  conceiving, combined with
  the talent of vividly
  reproducing these concepts
- the ability to represent
  objects, events or
  relationships not yet observed
- invention; creation

- fantasy
- erroneous belief; superstition.

This proves my point. A creation,
an erroneous belief.
The secret is revealed...
That's the promised land...
delivered.

Príncipe Vindouro

Well, what a journey…
The book will continue.
I want to make a division so that 'the first part' doesn't fall into the possibility of being a theory. I know it sounds audacious but should be considered as an absolute true inside the understanding.
I know it sound hypocrite at the same time. How am I saying that language is meaningless and there's no true and then, this…
I'm going to be honest, like I said through silence we can't explain anything, so this book is to explain the understanding through our invention. It's like when I came to the world was a game with some rules, but we say that the game is natural, so I found my way to find out about it.

From now on, I'm going to share a few texts from my notebook after I discovered all this, when I make some theories, wrote a few stories, some philosophical thoughts as well, with no topic in mind, just being bored and loving writing.

With that being said…

Thaumas

Thaumas, the father of Iris, the messenger of the gods who brought to men as a heavenly gift the love of wisdom (philosophia).

On the day I was made a believer that I was born, 19th of January, I lost my four-legged companion, Iris.
I cried and cried, locked in my room, her death opened the door to release what I had been accumulating for so long, my days were spent in frustration. I didn't understand why… What was the point of all this I called life?... Until I discovered the answer.
I discovered that it wasn't like

that. It's all just imagination and I must choose to believe in it… In birth… In death… and… if they take me to a place that slowly kills me, why bother or imagine that I have the knowledge of something that is just meanings, imagination. It's just stupid… But I've already said that I don't want to go back to nothingness… maybe to everything mean something… maybe so her passage in here don't be in vain… maybe to cry because is always a relieve… maybe because…

For Iris, the lovely 'meerkat'.

Adam and Eve

There are many different versions but from what I have researched I will briefly analyze the one I have always heard throughout my life. God created Adam from the dust and placed him in the Garden of Eden. He was told that he could freely eat from all the trees in the garden, except from the tree of knowledge of good and evil. Then, he created Eve from one of Adam's ribs to keep him company and the story proceeds with a serpent deceiving Eve into eating from the forbidden tree. Eve offers Adam the fruit, and God, knowing of the sin, curses the serpent and the earth and expels Adam and Eve from paradise.

So, I can associate this with what I explored in the book. My theory about this story is that couldn't be a paradise without the tree (good and evil), as without it, it would be devoid of meaning, the nothingness that I saw with the rule of infinity that later I substitute for the notion of life.

It is a sin to eat from the tree because from that moment, we become the main unit instead of life. That's why we were expelled... Paradise, when humans judge, will be impossible, each one of us can bring his concepts of good and evil according to a personal choice and not according to life, so there always be disagreement. It's not about one's life, but about the notion of life that we create as a whole.

I can go further and say that it was Eve who sinned because every mother wants the best for their offspring, selfishness, so it will go with personal choices of good and evil and not carrying about others life's. A little further and say that maybe they were not the first of their species to exist and instead the first to create a concept of a family.

Anyway...

Stories... It will never be more than that.

The secret always remains with those who write them.

Atlantis

Atlantis, the supposed advanced
society.

There are a thousand stories, so
this text will be just a thought
about it. Here's the thing: imagine
how advanced a civilization could
be where everyone knows what I
wrote in the book? A society
where there is no right knowledge
to be debated, each person knows
that is just an advanced
communication that we created
and the defined is accepted to have
a dream, to avoid nothingness.
Imagine the ideas that can arise...
every person with the power to
understand the dream, true equals.

I know these are just thoughts...

but I also know that identical statues are scattered worldwide at a time when, according to our history, shouldn't be there. My theory is that there was a society that created the notion of life we got today and spread it throughout the world to the point where even now (although divided into various languages, like the story of the tower of babel suggests), the meanings are all the same. You can notice that the notion of left, right, and even if there's no left and right there's a notion of directions so…

Oh well… theories… that's why I don't love them.

Chronos

Time. One belief that we humans have forgotten that we created and give as a certain. We always handle the same way the question about it, if exists or not, and no matter how many years go by, nothing gets resolved and to be honest, we get deeper into it.

First, I will see what the dictionary says about it.

Time:
- the succession of moments in which events unfold
- part of the duration occupied by events
- a continuous and undefined period in which events follow one another; duration
- the era in which one lives

- limited duration (in opposition to the concept of eternity)

Now... there are three groups in society regarding the question of whether time exists or not. Those who don't care, although their life is governed by the definition that exists. Those who study it and consider it as reality, and finally, those who think they are not believers but when asked why, they shrug their shoulders and say things like, 'only the moment exists' as if the word moment is not about time.

So, the time I will write about here is the one from the group that studies it and consider as reality, and I will call it the true time to distinguish it from the one they created more blatantly for mass control, the false time, where hours, days, and years exist. The true time is the one that, no matter how much one tries to deny, seems impossible. Science itself has mixed filling about it, it's important for most of the accounts they have but at the same time can almost admit is just something that the brain sees to make the understanding easier.

I understand the confusion... it becomes difficult to deny when we notice something happening from birth to death. From this, we could conclude that it is just a unit of measurement, although its existence is not denied yet. It is a question that has not being made for long, the existence of both times been around since Greek mythology when themselves were knowledgeable about Chronos and Kairos.

I can prove that it does not exist, solve the enigma that has lasted since humans ceased to understand their own inventions, and for that, I must go back to the same topic I refer to on 'the first part'.

Our understanding of something is our invention. We the ones who name it, give it a definition, and that creates a belief. Then, we teach it, it will be passed down from generation to generation and when we forget that we named it and gave it a definition, it becomes reality.

I'll take the part of the dictionary that mentions limited duration (in opposition to the concept of eternity). Therefore, here we have the concept of birth and death,

which I think we take as reality
when in fact, it is obvious that the
universe did not whisper 'look,
that's called birth' or 'that's death'.
It was us, humans, who named it
and gave it a definition on what is
birth and death. Vision is one of
the main reasons that lead us to
believe that it is 'real', but as
Socrates said and Plato wrote 'we
use our eyes to see' meaning that
something else uses it, and it is
that something else that we are
and use to approve concepts.
 So, if the concepts of birth and
death are inventions, why wouldn't
the unit that measures the middle
not be? Actually, everything is.
Even if we have a biological side
is what I define as the natural side,
rational, or whatever we want to
call it. On the other side, the

advanced communication that allows thinking, is simply a creation through imagination of all the meanings of everything. Unfortunately, what we design as 'reality' is out of sense.

The proof of this can be found in a play as an example. If it represents a time when people lived, what distinguishes it from reality is simply that at the time it represents, they had the belief that it was like that. In the play, the actors must pretend to be like that because their belief of how it is in the outside world has already changed.

One of the things that motivated me to delve into this issue to find an answer for it was a child who was at a party in my former workplace. The party lasted three hours and she came up to me, very happy, and asked "how long until the party ends?". I answered an hour and a half, and received the question back "how long is an hour and a half?" And... well... how do I explain to the child? Actually, how do I explain even to myself? Would anyone be satisfied if the answer were just 'it's the time it takes to get from here to there?' or should I explain that we create the concept of space and to measure the concept of time? I wanted an explanation for myself as well, and here it is.

I hope it runs around the world one day and helps others too. Oh... if you think it wasn't well explained, think about the part of understanding and if you feel that as a singularity, you are better than someone else to assert with certainty that something is the definition of anything. If you don't, don't worry… nobody should be. If you do, I would also like to have that personal conversation with the universe.

Science

The concept of science is also something that is not debated nowadays. Every human trust it, as it is part of our rational side, and although some may distrust it, to be honest, it is often too irrational.

I will write about science, excluding the medical side, as I have seen in the book that it aligns with the discussion of good and evil about life so, there's not much discussion about it, of course it will be good because makes life longer and a disease kills, bla, bla, bla. The equation, according to life, always.

Therefore, the science that I will write about it is the one that is vague, and I consider kind of unimportant but unfortunately, we see it as a guarantee for humanity's path, our future. Actually, it's difficult for me to think about how in Plato's book (Theaetetus), Socrates analyses all the thinking about what science is and doesn't reach any conclusion, but when I open a simple dictionary nowadays... there it is. This bothers me a little, so I will point out some things about it as well, as a philosophic thought.

I will start with, isn't our knowledge in a universe that we believe to be vast an insult to that same vastness? An example that I like to think that includes the vastness we believe in, is the fact that people like to wonder if there is life on other planets without ever questioning where the concept of life comes from. Even if there was life outside the planet... why do people think they could communicate if they even can't understand a dog's bark? If we communicate with the dog, it's because the dog obeys us and understands what we're saying, not the other way around. However, we are supposed to be the intelligent species, right? Ironic. What makes us believe as well that life outside our planet will have accomplished the same understanding as us?

Being honest, do we really think we are discovering something about the universe when we name things like gravity and calculate it with the numbers, that we created to get results that... sorry to inform you, if we want to call it knowledge and facts, fine, but it will always be what we wanted to be. It is not a certainty.

To make a point, in my adolescence I made a draw showing various planets, and from those planets, a hologram like image of their understanding emerged on top of each planet. On Earth, I wrote a few words, and on the other planets I randomly invented something to show on top as well. The question I wrote in the corner of the drawing was: 'what is the right imagination?'. Given that each planet has its own will be unfair for one to say that its meanings are the right ones.

We should understand that we invented and later think we discovered.

An example of how certain

information that we consider important in science is insignificant is Copernicus' discovery for instance, when he found that the sun is the center of the solar system. I could show him respect... but how did he never realized that the definition of center, revolves, the solar system itself, are concepts invented by us? Especially let me point out that such information did not help humans in any concrete way to be honest.

All this science is possible because we no longer ask the question that should be asked: are humans the main unit? Doesn't sound like narcissism? Not even a little? Note that if humans are considered the main unit, it already kind of proves that all understanding is just our imagination working and we consider imagination as something not real.

It may sound ridiculous but that's where we are right now.

The reason science does not question the fact that we are the main unit is because without it, science wouldn't even be possible since nothing could be given as a certain.

In conclusion... We cannot forget that theories are not facts and fact is just a word, can 'prove' something inside of the understanding but the understanding, again, is just a creation through imagination.

So, until now in humanity all we have is assumptions, and assumptions cannot be the path to the 'truth' we've been looking for. It is better to admit that we don't know than to invent things that we can't prove and will never be able to do so.

Whatever science is, had been on a wrong path. How can we explain that there are people who do not have the necessary to live, yet we are funding and idolizing those who suppose what is inside a black hole? To be honest… the spiritual path of religion is preferable over the factual path of science.

Science invented a dice from one to six, and only lose when the dice shows above six.

Anyway…

Religion

Nowadays, religion is not even a matter of discussion.

There are fanatics, non-believers who consider themselves people of science, and non-believers because it has become fashionable to associate religion with a lack of intelligence.

Believing in the existence of a higher power is normal. In fact, it gives a justification to good and evil (even though I don't agree with it) shows more intelligence than factual science.

The books that represent each religion are taken too literally and should not. We must learn to take metaphors, just as we do with any other stories, and stop pointing out, especially atheists, the fantasy. In the example of the story of Moses. The story shows a people who suffered immensely from slave labor and were freed by passing through the sea that Moses divided in two. It should be an example of what to do and what to fight for rather than focusing on the idea that it didn't happen because Moses didn't split the sea in half. Well, sorry to inform… the story of Alice in Wonderland says that Alice was chasing a rabbit dressed in a large watch, and it's a lie as well. However, it does contain beautiful metaphors about life, so we can read and point out that rather than point the fantasy, right?

The story of Jesus of Nazareth. A man who wanted to show the people what really mattered by fighting against the tax and helping to combat poverty. What do we take away from the story? That it is impossible for someone to turn water into wine and that his mother was not a virgin because that is scientifically impossible. Nobody talks about the important parts of the story but instead it seems to be more convenient to focus on what is scientifically possible or not.

I know that there are many religions and I have only written about Christianity. I'm sorry but I'm not an expert about it and I grew up in a Cristian country, but I'll try to write more globally in the remaining few lines.

We should not confuse the true religion with the false religion that humans take advantage of to profit and torment poor souls. True religion is something that was created to complement the dream, while the false religion was something that was created for someone to control the dream.

I know that in the past, people were burned for having different beliefs, but the state also arrests people and science has its experiments as well. These three are just concepts, and of course, in the wrong hands, they will work the other way of the purpose of their creation.

Religion is the most reliable path. Even if someone wants to gather information, as science does, there will come a day when the decision must be made on the spiritual side. For example, I hear talk about overpopulation in the world, that there are too many of us and it will be difficult to live on this planet. Therefore, if we go by the facts (since science cannot prove good and evil), reducing the population will be the step to take, right? but no one wants to be treated like a number when it comes to creating a way to do, so… What do we really want?

It's time to stop being an atheist just because it's trendy or thinking that we are superior for not believing in. Some believe they die and go to heaven and while others ridicule the idea of heaven, they are still believers in what death is, and… it's all the same... imagination.

Complex

How many more trips around the sun until we arrive on what we pretend?

What is the point of increasing life expectancy if we spend most of it working for a world that we don't even think about?

Studying, working, being grateful for the opportunity because there are those who do not have food or a place to sleep. It seems that the goal is to make us feel like guests on a planet that was supposed to be ours, not someone else's, and one of the worst part is that we are made to believe that nothing exists without that someone else.

We are asked to entertain ourselves by earning a piece of paper, spending it on visiting another piece of land with a different name where monuments were built as an order of someone, probably built with little enthusiasm since it was an order.

We date our beliefs, later we name them as an era, but nothing changes except for the belief we hold. Even if there is a possibility in science to achieve what we want, I believe that the day will come when we are faced with the question of what to do with the rest of time that we face to raise our children healthily.

Please tell me that someone is thinking about this... Are we just doing things for the sake of doing them?...

Those who give orders do not suffer... They sit accumulating the paper they love so much, that's why they ask for it back. It irritates me. I know I'm not the only one tired of waking up five days a week to the irritating sound in my ear, having to leave the house in torrential rain, as if this was the purpose of having created the dream. It was supposed to bring comfort to the world without having to conquer it, and instead, we are moving away from the fire that we start to control to feel safe, to earn a paper that can buy it.

It sounds so ridiculous…

We divide the world to make it perfectly clear which path to follow: from third world to second to first. We offer schools and the opportunity to dream freely in all of them, but the third and second one, we'll see in the first if we like the way they behave. It's shameful... Some places don't even have access to clean water, and yet in places like Portugal, we got the bidet because sometimes our feet get dirty, and we find it disgusting.

Anyway...

It's not funny, but I find it amusing...

We deflect attention away from all of this… We love the word 'complex'. It allows us to escape, and it justifies it for the time being. We never admit that we are the creators, leaving room for us to 'discover' because we are intelligent and everything is super complex, right?

Thus, the phrase of Jesus on the way to the cross now makes sense to me. "Father, forgive them, for they know not what they do.".

The end

Printed in Great Britain
by Amazon